PRAYER

COMMUNICATION WITH OUR FATHER

MINISTER
ROBERT JOHNSON

ISBN 979-8-89526-638-0 (paperback)
ISBN 979-8-89526-639-7 (digital)

Christian Faith Publishing
832 Park Avenue
Meadville, PA 16335
www.christianfaithpublishing.com

Printed in the United States of America

Let my prayer be set forth before thee
as incense; and the lifting up of my
hands as the evening sacrifice.

—Psalm 141:2

This book on prayer is dedicated to my wife,
Mary, the members of Word of Faith and the
body (church) of our Lord Jesus Christ.

CONTENTS

Introduction...ix
Prayer Our Spiritual Weapon 1
Jesus Our Mediator 6
  You must have faith......................................9
  Humble prayer..11
  Temple versus house of prayer................12
  Praise, Worship, and Thanksgiving........13
Pray Always...15
What Do We Pray For? 21
Worldliness 24
Exhortation to Pray 28
  Head covering for women.........................30
  Name it and claim it 37
  Public versus private prayer....................38
  Cursing or blessing.....................................40
Intercession 45
  His will be done...51
In Jesus's Name..54
Fasting..57
  Mental illness...62
Praying in Tongues 65
Conclusion...67
  Does The Most High still speak 69
  Do not trust your heart.............................71

INTRODUCTION

This is a serious work on prayer. This small book is for serious saints and not for the casual saint. If you are a serious saint, you will look up all scripture verses given. We are commanded to take prayer very seriously. Prayer is not a spiritual gift; it is a requirement. Prayer is part of our spiritual warfare. We are commanded to pray without ceasing. But many of us find prayer difficult and hard. My goal is to help each of us overcome this hurdle. This is not a teaching about writing your own ticket with The Most High. He is not our sugar daddy waiting to meet our every want. And this is not an attempt to make excuses for The Most High; He does what He knows is right. I have used scriptures as the basis for this teaching. I believe only scriptures should be used to teach spiritual principles and not man made doctrines.

Let us define the word *pray*.

Prayer/Supplication: an earnest oratory, communication, verbally given, beg, urgent, earnestly given, worshipful request, petition, approach for a favor, beseech made to The Most High. (*Strong's Exhaustive Concordance of the Bible*. Thomas Nelson Publishers, 2010)

Notice the word *communication* is included in the definition. Prayer is communication with The Most High.

> After this manner therefore pray ye; Our Father which are in heaven. (Matthew 6:9)

Jesus and John taught their disciples to pray.

> And it came to pass, that as he was praying in a
> certain place, when he ceased, one of his disciples
> said unto him, "Lord, teach us to pray, as John
> also taught his disciples." (Luke 11:1)

This verse teaches me that some aspects of prayer must be taught. That is the goal of this small book—that we may learn to pray.

If, after reading this book, you can honestly say you have nothing to pray for, it is obvious you do not know The Most High. And if you are comfortable just praying the Lord's prayer every day, this book is not for you.

I am going to teach some strong truths against some of our most cherished beliefs. Do not get angry, but get your Bible and see if those things that are taught are true. Our goal is to dispel myths and other false ideas satan and ourselves have allowed to creep into praying. We have all seen the picture of the so-called Christ in the garden with His hands folded together praying. We have no scripture basis for this. This is a man-made depiction with no basis in scripture.

We close our eyes, hold hands, and fold our hands together, placing them before our faces, thinking this is the way to pray. I have seen saints wave their hands over or towards people. That is mysticism or magic (2 Kings 5:11). There is no biblical basis for this. Saints also talk about a "point of contact, to release your faith." This, too, is a fallacy given by preachers. I challenge anyone to show me this "point of contact, to release your faith" teaching in the Bible. Your faith does not depend on a "point of contact." Your faith depends on you believing The Most High. Do not walk after the vanity of your mind (Ephesians 4:17–19).

Jesus's garment was touched (Matthew 14:36–37). Jesus did lay His hands on many, and they were healed (Mark 1:40–45), and handkerchiefs were sent out from Paul (Acts 19:12, no money involved). But these do not establish this teaching. I remember seeing preachers telling folks to run and touch their TV or the radio as a "point of contact" or send them $20.00 to get the miracle faith cloth. These are gimmicks used by charlatans to separate you from your money. Prayer has no gimmicks.

You should not pray to or have any picture of a so-called Christ. You should most definitely get rid of any pictures you may have of Christ, even the ones in your church. One, we should not have pictures of Christ, for He is God (Exodus 20:1–6; Deuteronomy 4:15–16; John 1:1–4; Romans 1:21–25). Two, we have no idea what He looks like other than the description given in Revelation chapter 1. The rest are traditions men have put into the system. We walk by faith, and anything not of faith is sin (Romans 14:23). With this work, we are not trying to throw everything out, but if it is dead, useless, and nonproductive, what good is it? We must get rid of all hindrances to our prayers.

> For therein is the righteousness of God revealed
> from faith to faith: for it is written, The just shall
> live by faith. (Romans 1:17)

> For we walk by faith, not by sight. (2 Corinthians
> 5:7)

Listen, do you really understand what that verse means? As Christians, we have no holy sites, no holy water. Everything we need has been supplied by Christ; we need nothing else. We are the holy sites of God (2 Corinthians 6:16). So wherever we are, as the temples of The Most High, we make that spot holy.

I want you to stop reading this and go and read the following scriptures for yourself; Genesis 18:14; Jeremiah 32:17, 27; Matthew 19:26; Mark 10:27; and Luke 1:37. All these verses have one thing in common: nothing is too hard for The Most High.

Prayer is communication with our Father; if you are not praying, you are not communicating. Almost every book of the New Testament mentions a form of the word *pray, prayers, prayed,* or *praying.* Prayer is held in high esteem and is particularly important to The Most High. I am not an expert; I struggle just like you to pray.

My goal is to encourage us to pray and hopefully help our prayers be effective, enjoyable, and in accordance with our Father's will. Many saints look at prayer as a formality, just something we are supposed to do, and do not really expect answers to their prayers.

> Epaphras, who is one of you, servant of Christ, saluteth you, always laboring fervently for you in prayers, that you may stand perfect and complete in all the will of God. (Colossians 4:12)

> And this is the confidence that we have in him, that, if we ask any thing according, to his will, he heareth us. (1 John 5:14)

Notice Epaphras labored fervently in prayer for the Colossians to stand perfect and complete in all the will of The Most High. And then The Father tells us through John to ask according to His will. This says His will be done, not ours. Do you know The Father's will? If not, then you need to read and study His word. We have too many stupid saints. I know this is a harsh word but The Most High used it. Read on:

> For my people is foolish, they have not known me; they are scottish children, and they have none understanding: they are wise to do evil, but to do good they have no knowledge. (Jeremiah 4:22)

The word *scottish* in the above verse means stupid. The Most High is not insulting us but telling the truth. Saints are some of the most ignorant and gullible people when it comes to knowledge about The Most High. All some male or female preacher has to do is twist the scripture and throw a spiritual idea on it, and most Christians scream hallelujah. But yet that so-called great revelation does not work for them. This is what they want to hear because they have itching ears that need to be scratched with soothing fleshly words. This is why so many saints listen to and are deceived by false teachers.

> That we henceforth be no more children, tossed to and fro, and carried about with every wind of doctrine, by the sleight (cleverness) of men, and cunning craftiness (tricks), whereby they lie in wait to deceive. (Ephesians 4:14)

There are people and demons out there who want to intentionally deceive you. Let no faith healer convince you to throw away your medicines or stop going to the doctors as an act of faith. The Most High can heal with or without medicine or doctors. Be careful when making vows as you pray. Do not promise how good you are going to be; just ask forgiveness and pray.

Let us get further into our study. I will write out most scriptures we will be using. I have added parentheses ( ), when I want to clarify some scriptures. I am not adding, just clarifying those scriptures. And I will capitalize all pronouns that reference The Most High and our Savior. I will also lowercase satan's name. All scriptures are from the King James Version (KJV) of the Bible. I also encourage scripture memorization using the KJV for a time of need. The KJV has a cadence that lends it to memorization. The other Bible interpretations do not have this. All scriptures will be in a block paragraph. AI was not used in writing this book.

PRAYER OUR SPIRITUAL WEAPON

Praying always with all prayer and supplication in the Spirit, and watching thereunto with all perseverance and supplication for all saints. (Ephesians 6:18)

For though we walk in the flesh, we do not war after the flesh: (For the weapons of our warfare are not carnal but mighty through God to the pulling down of strongholds;) Casting down imagination, and every high thing that exalts itself against the knowledge of God, and bringing into captivity every thought to the obedience of Christ; and having in a readiness to revenge all disobedience, when your obedience is fulfilled. (2 Corinthians 10:3–6)

There is therefore now no condemnation to them which are in Christ Jesus who walk not after the flesh, but after the Spirit. (Romans 8:1)

We are to walk in the ways of the Bible. The Bible is a spiritual book full of what a spiritual God says. So as much as is in you, walk in what the Bible teaches us. Jesus took the word very seriously. He told

John the Baptist that John had to baptize Him to fulfill all righteousness (Matthew 3:15).

Prayer is a spiritual weapon to be used in the spiritual realm. To fight someone after the flesh is futile. You must fight in the spiritual realm, and that is where prayer comes in.

I am going to give a short study on spiritual warfare. I want you to read Daniel chapter 10 first. I am going to give a short synopsis of the chapter. Daniel had been fasting and praying for twenty-one days in an attempt to gain understanding concerning the interpretation of a vision he was given.

An angel from The Most High was sent to reveal the interpretation to Daniel on the very first day of his fasting and prayer. However, the evil angel that governed over the kingdom of Persia hindered the Lord's angel from getting to Daniel. The Medo-Persian empire had conquered Babylon (Daniel 5:22–31).

The angel needed help from Michael, one of the archangels, to help him fight the evil angel of Persia. Once they defeated this evil angel, then the angel could continue on his mission to give Daniel the interpretation. The angel then told Daniel that he would have to return and fight the evil angel over Grecia that was to come after Persia was defeated. If you are a history buff, you would know at this time that the Medo-Persian kingdom was being ruled through Darius the Mede and Cyrus the Persian and that Alexander the Great, ruler of Greece, would defeat the Medo-Persian empire and capture Babylon.

You may be thinking this story is far-fetched, but it is true. The Most High sometimes use spiritual events to manifest earthly situations. This is not the only passage that illustrates spiritual warfare. First Chronicles 21:1–30 tells how satan influenced King David to disobey the command not to number Israel. The Most High punished King David by sending an angel to slay seventy thousand people. Verses 14–16 say it was an angel, but it manifested as a pestilence upon the people.

In 2 Chronicles 18:18–23, one spirit was allowed to influence four hundred of King Ahab's yes prophets in order for Ahab to die. The Most High could have just taken King Ahab's breath, but He didn't, and those prophets did not have to follow the spirit but chose to follow the lie that was placed into their minds. This was not a lying spirit, whose sole job was to put lies in people's minds. All evil spirits lie (John 8:44); that is their nature.

> And with all deceivableness of unrighteousness in them that perish; because they received not the love of the truth, that they might be saved. And for this because God shall send them strong delusion, that they should believe a lie. (2 Thessalonians 2:10–11)

Even in the New Testament, Acts 12:20–25, an angel smote King Herold, but it was manifested as worms eating him. There are others, but we cannot explore them now. Second Chronicles 20:20–30 and 2 Chronicles 21:18–20, to name a few. We have become so sophisticated that we fail to see what is going on around us. Please understand I am not trying to spiritualize every event. There is not a demon behind every rock waiting to get you, but we are spirit beings in fleshly bodies in an evil world populated with spiritually evil angels.

Let none of this upset you; remember, The Most High is sovereign, just, and will always do right. None can judge, scorn, or admonish Him.

> To the intent that now unto the principalities and powers in heavenly places might be known by the church the manifold wisdom of God. (Ephesians 3:10)

> Put on the whole armor of God, that you may be able to stand against the Wiles of the devil. For we wrestle not against flesh and blood, but against principalities, against powers, against the rulers of the darkness of this world, against

spiritual wickedness in high places. (Ephesians
6:11–12)

Have you ever wondered why many government leaders make the same mistakes as their predecessors? Spiritual warfare. Those same evil angels are there to influence him or her into doing the same evil as their predecessors. Many leaders have tried communism over and over, and it has never worked. Communism has done nothing but cause misery for millions. So why do they keep trying? Evil spiritual influence. We must pray that these leaders will follow God's influences. Instead of talking against the ruler, pray for them to be saved (Acts 23:1–5).

We serve a spiritual God who does use the spiritual realm to bring things into this fleshly world. Do not let these verses confuse you. But remember, He is omnipotent and can do whatever He deems necessary. In some instances, He makes things just happen; in others, He uses people or events to do His will upon this earth.

Remember the former things of old: for I am God
and there is none else; I am God, and there is
none like me. Declaring the end from the begin-
ning, and from ancient times the things that are
not yet done, saying, my counsel shall stand and
I will do all my pleasure: calling a ravenous bird
from the east, the man that executeth my counsel
from a far country: yea, I have spoken it, I will
also bring it to pass; I have purposed it, I will also
do it. (Isaiah 46:9–11)

Remember, this world is temporarily satan's kingdom (John 14:30, 12:31) and he did not fall by himself; one third of the angels rebelled with him. satan is a created being and cannot control this world by himself; thus, he has evil angels over different nations trying to control those nations. I used the word trying because man is a very stubborn and rebellious subject. So satan needs help. This is why we must pray for our leaders to oppose the evil influence of the devil and his angels as they try to work their evil on them.

Let me add this here: a true Christian cannot be demon-possessed. The Holy Spirit and demons cannot be in the same body at the same time. The enemy tries to oppress and influence all of us, but that is not a demonic possession. The devil and demons cannot read your mind. That would make them equal with The Most High. They can send thoughts to your mind, as satan did with King David in 1 Chronicles 21:1.

Remember this: be careful how you deal with the satan. He is not old slewfoot, pointy-head, or any other nickname. He does not wear a red suit and carry a pitchfork. The unclean angels that fell with him are not little imps or trolls. They are the enemy of our soul. And he wants you to make fun of him and his demons. Because anything you can laugh at, you do not take seriously. Do not fear him or his demons. Greater is He that is in you than he that is in the world. Have you ever heard that before?

> But if our gospel be hid, it is hid to them that are lost: In whom the god of this world hath blinded the minds of them which believed not, lest the light of the glorious gospel of Christ, who is the image of God, should shine unto them. (2 Corinthians 4:3–4)

Saints, we must not allow the enemy to blind our minds. Do not let Hollywood dictate what you believe about the spiritual world. Because 99.99 percent of what is portrayed in Hollywood is wrong. We must trust The Most High, whether we understand His actions or not. I am amazed that The Most High has given me a part in what happens in this world through my prayers. Pray, saints, and never give up.

JESUS OUR MEDIATOR

> For there is one God, and one mediator between God and men, the man Christ Jesus. (1 Timothy 2:5)

> And for this cause he is the mediator of the new testament, that by means of death, for the redemption of the transgressions that were under the first testament, they which are called might receive the promise of eternal inheritance. (Hebrews 9:15)

This means that in heaven there is only one intercessor between us and The Most High; His name is Christ. Prayers are never ever directed toward angels. Angels are created beings, so why would you pray to them? Nowhere in the Bible will you find anyone directing prayers to angels. Do not seek angels. You cannot dispatch angels to bring you money or property. Angels cannot forgive sin. Read Exodus 23:20–22. Angels are ministering spirits at the sole command of The Most High. Do not seek angels. Seek The Most High.

> Let no man beguile you of your reward in a voluntary humility and worshiping of angels, intruding into those things which he have not seen, vainly puffed up by his fleshly mind. (Colossians 2:18)

> For such are false prophets, deceitful workers,
> transforming themselves into the apostles of Christ.
> And no marvel; For Satan himself is transformed
> into an angel of light. Therefore, it is no great thing
> if his ministers also be transformed as the ministers
> of righteousness; who's end shall be according to
> their works. (2 Corinthians 11:13–15)

So-called biblical teachers who teach this doctrine concerning angels are really intruding into areas that are not taught in the Bible. They are using their fleshly minds to produce such non-biblical teaching. Just as satan deceives people into believing lies, so do his ministers.

Any prayer directed toward any dead person, no matter how great a life they lived before death, is unbiblical, and it is sin. They can do nothing for you. Even though people claim healing because they prayed to some dead person, that is not a valid reason for you to pray to them. This includes praying to statues. A few years ago, my wife and I went to Utah, and we went to the Mormon Temple Square. We went into one of their historic buildings. And there we saw an eleven-foot-tall white Carrara marble statue of their so-called Jesus. Sitting in front of that statue was a group of tourists from Japan, and they were worshipping this hunk of rock. Their eyes were full of tears as they prayed to this rock idol. This is blasphemy.

Just because you received an answer to your prayer does not mean it came because you prayed to a good dead person, a statue, or other idol. Remember, all things come from our Father, and He gives the unsaved mercy also.

> That you may be the children of your Father
> which is in heaven: for he maketh his sun to rise
> on the evil and on the good, and sendeth rain on
> the just and on the unjust. (Matthew 5:45)

Our Father is merciful and heals as He wills. And because of Christ's atoning work for us, we can come boldly to the throne of grace with our prayers (Hebrews 10:19).

Prayers to Mary, Jesus's earthly mother, are a waste of your time. She cannot answer or intercede on your behalf. Neither she nor any other dead saint in heaven are co-intercessors with Christ. No organization can declare someone a saint. When you get saved, you are now a saint or set apart one (Psalm 89:5; Acts 26:10; Philippians 1:1, 4:2; Colossians 1:2; and Romans 1:7). Never ever direct your prayers to any dead person. Your dead ancestors cannot hear your prayers or do anything for you, and if you face the fact, some of them are actually in hell. You are setting yourself up to be fooled by demons. Please do not go to Sister Rosa or Brother Big Daddy Slick to get a word from The Most High or your ancestors, because you are communicating with demons.

This same principle is used in praying to the stars and planets And consulting your so-called horoscope. Why would you do this? All of this is foolishness. They were all created by and for The Most High. Seek The Most High while He may be found.

One of the most important things about prayer is to pray in your own words. Just do it. Prayer is especially important, or else it would not be mentioned so often. You do not need a prayer app, a prayer book, prayer beads, or AI to help you pray. It is not to be a rote, habitual recital of words. You should use scripture such as the Psalms to help you pray, but stay away from prewritten prayers. Many of them are unscriptural and are written by unsaved writers for money.

In 2010, I was shot six times in the abdomen and chest area in an assassination attempt at my home on the orders of the Crips prison leadership. I was the captain of the contraband section at Lee State Prison. I fell into the bathroom, sat against the bathtub, and began to quote scriptures. A couple of the scriptures I quoted were:

> I shall not die, but live, and declare the works of the Lord. (Psalm 118:17)

> No weapon that is formed against thee shall prosper; and every tongue that shall rise against thee in judgment thou shalt condemn, this is the heritage of the servants of the Lord, and their righteousness is of me, saith the lord. (Isaiah 54:17)

I used these and many other scriptures as my prayers. I did not think, *Lord, let me live.* I quoted scriptures as my prayers. If you wish to read more on this shooting, get the book *On Point!: The Making of a Prison Contraband Captain* by Captain Robert Johnson.

YOU MUST HAVE FAITH

. . . . .

Jesus said, "…for your Father, knoweth what things ye have need of, before ye ask him." (Matthew 6:8)

The Father knows what we need because He is Omniscient or all-knowing. And He is concerned about your needs. So our question is, since He is all-knowing, why should I pray for my needs? The answer is that He told us to pray. You do not ask someone for something if you do not believe that person can give what you ask. We are told in:

But without faith it is impossible to please him: for he that cometh to God must believe that he is, and that he is a rewarder of them that diligently seek him. (Hebrews 11:6)

In the New Testament, when some people came to Jesus for healing, He asked them, "Do you believe I can do this?" Or He said, "According to your faith."

Prayer shows you believe (have faith) in Him and that He has the ability to give you what you need as you work hard (diligently) to seek Him. He will reward you in His way. Do not allow doubt to enter your prayer life.

But let him ask in faith, nothing waving. For he that wavereth is like a wave of the sea driven with the wind and tossed. For let not that man

think that he shall receive anything of the Lord.
A double-minded man is unstable in all his ways.
(James 1:6–8)

You just trust and leave the outcome to Him.

Trust in the Lord with all thine heart; and lean
not unto thine own understanding. In all thy
ways acknowledge him and he shall direct thy
paths. (Proverbs 3:5–6)

Prayer shows you trust Him, are not leaning to your own
devices, and are willing to follow His leading. Prayer shows we trust
Him for all things and trust ourselves for nothing.

Behold, the Lord's hand is not shortened, that it
cannot save; neither his ear heavy, that it cannot
hear: but your iniquities have separated between
you and your God, and your sins have hid his face
from you, that he will not hear. (Isaiah 59:1–2)

If my people, which are called by my name, shall
humble themselves, and pray, and seek my face,
and turn from their wicked ways; Then will I
hear from heaven, and will forgive their sin, and
will heal their land. (2 Chronicles 7:14)

If I regard iniquity in my heart, the Lord will not
hear me. (Psalm 66:18)

The Lord is far from the wicked: but he heareth
the prayer of the righteous. (Proverbs 15:29)

The above verses show we must seek forgiveness of our favorite
sins before coming to Him in prayer. Always ask forgiveness so that
nothing is between Him and you.

HUMBLE PRAYER

. . . . .

Beware of pride; of all the sins there are, *pride* is number one. Our Father hates pride. All sins are based on pride. We fight to do it our way, not His way. The two highest of His creation fell due to pride, lucifer and Adam. Prayer must be made with an attitude of humbleness.

> And be clothed with humility: for God resisteth the proud, and giveth grace to the humble. (1 Peter 5:5b)

> And he spake this parable unto certain which trusted in themselves that they were righteous and despised others; two men went up into the temple to pray; The one a pharisee, the other a publican. The Pharisee stood and prayed thus with himself, God, I thank thee, that I am not as other men are, extortioners, unjust, adulterers, or even as this publican. I fast twice in the week I give tithes of all that I possess. And the publican standing far off would not lift up so much as his eyes unto heaven, but smote upon his breast, saying God be merciful unto me a sinner. I tell you this man went down to his house justified rather than the other: for everyone that exalteth himself shall be abased; and he that humbles himself shall be exalted. (Luke 18:9–14)

There is much to learn in this text. Do not brag on yourself to The Most High, because He knows the truth about you. Notice the Pharisee prayed with "himself." His prayer went nowhere. Whereas the publican could not look up, he just hit himself on the chest and said, "God, be merciful to me a, sinner." Which one do you think The Most High heard?

> These six things doth the Lord hate: yea, seven are an abomination unto him, a proud look, a lying tongue, and hands that shed innocent blood, a heart that deviseth wicked imaginations, feet that be swift in running to mischief, a false witness that speaketh lies, and he that soweth discord among brethren. (Proverbs 6:16–19)

If you examine the above verses, you will see each and every one of the sins listed has pride at their base. I cannot emphasize it enough. The Most High hates pride.

> "For from within, out of the heart of men, proceed evil thoughts, adulteries, fornications, murders. Thefts, covetousness, wickedness, deceit, lasciviousness, and evil eye, blasphemy, *pride*, foolishness; all these evil things come from within and defile the man." (Mark 7:21)

TEMPLE VERSUS HOUSE OF PRAYER

In Isaiah 56:7 and Luke 19:45–46, The Most High referred to the temple as His house of prayer. But now those who are saved are His houses of prayer.

> Jesus answered and said unto him, if a man love me, he will keep my words: and my Father will love him, and we will come unto him, and make our abode with him. (John 14:23)

What? Know you not that your body is the temple of the Holy Ghost, which is in you, which you have of God, and ye are not your own. (1 Corinthians 6:19)

Ye also, as lively stones, are built up a spiritual house, a holy priesthood, to offer up spiritual sacrifices, acceptable to God by Jesus Christ. (1 Peter 2:5)

We are His living temples, and as such, we must be a house of prayer. Notice we have been made acceptable to God by Jesus Christ. Nothing we do other than depend on Christ makes us acceptable to The Most High.

PRAISE, WORSHIP, AND THANKSGIVING

As you prepare to pray, you should always come before Him with praise, worship, and thanksgiving.

Enter into his gates with thanksgiving, and into his courts with praise: be thankful unto him, and bless his name. (Psalm 100:4)

PRAISE ye the Lord: for it is good to sing praise unto our God; for it is pleasant; and praise is comely (appropriate). (Psalm 147:1)

O GIVE thanks unto the Lord for he is good for his mercy endureth forever. (Psalm 107:1)

Let us talk about *thanksgiving*. When we close our prayer, we should always give Him thanksgiving. Many church folks close their prayer in the following manner: "We thank You for these and other blessings." Try dropping the "other blessings." And just say, "We thank You for this opportunity to pray," or something to that effect. Also sometimes try a prayer of nothing but thanksgiving. Isn't that a novel idea? Just thank Him for His goodness instead of asking.

PRAY ALWAYS

The position of prayer is not important. Biblical people prayed sitting, lying face down, kneeling, kneeling with their face in between their knees. Some prayed standing, looking up to heaven, or looking down to the ground. Your eyes do not have to be close to communicate with our Father. Daniel prayed facing Jerusalem. He also prayed three times a day; King David also prayed multiple times each day. I find no standard number or position. Just pray.

You do not need flowery words to impress The Most High. We pray to Him and not to impress others nor show our command of the language; we are praying to The Most High. You do not have to pray using the old English words thy, thee, and thou. The Most High does not use King James English. Sometimes when I pray in a public setting, I cringe when I hear people say to me, "What a great prayer that was." I was not praying to them, nor was I looking for their approval. I feel as if they have messed the prayer up because they have given me their approval, which I was not seeking.

> And he spake a parable unto them to this end, that
> men ought always to pray, and not to faint…And
> the Lord said, Hear what the unjust judge saith.
> And shall not God avenge his own elect, which cry
> day and night unto him though he bear long with
> them? I tell you that he will avenge them speedily.
> Nevertheless, when the Son of man cometh, shall
> he find faith on the earth? (Luke 18:1, 6–8)

God, who at sundry times and in divers manners spake in time past unto the fathers by the prophets, hath in these last days spoken unto us by his Son, whom he hath appointed heir of all things, by whom also he made the worlds. (Hebrews 1:1–2)

Therefore we ought to give the more earnest heed to the things which we have heard, least at any time we should let them slip. For the word spoken by angels was steadfast, and every transgression and disobedience received a just recompense of reward; how shall we escape, if we neglect so great salvation; Which at the first began to be spoken by the Lord, and was confirmed unto us by them that heard him. (Hebrews 2:1–3)

Jesus commands us to pray. His coming to the earth started the last days, which we are now in. It is imperative we give heed to what He is saying to us. Prayer to The Most High shows Him and us that we have faith in Him. We must never cease praying as long as we are able to utter a word. "Nevertheless, when the Son of Man cometh, shall he find faith (prayer) on the earth." Never allow yourself to grow weary in praying.

And Lest I should be exalted above measure through the abundance of the revelation, there was given to me a thorn in the flesh, the messenger of Satan to buffet me, lest I should be exalted above measure. For this thing I've besought the Lord thrice that it might depart from me. And he said unto me, my grace is sufficient for thee: for my strength is made perfect in weakness. Most gladly therefore will I glory in my infirmities, that the power of Christ may rest upon me. Therefore, I take pleasure in infirmities, in reproaches, in necessities, in persecutions, in distresses for Christ's sake: for when I am weak then am I strong. (2 Corinthians 12:7–10)

If what you are seeking has not come forth yet, do not faint or lose heart. Trust The Most High.

Pray without ceasing. (1 Thessalonians 5:17)

Those three words, along with what Jesus said, teach us that we must never stop praying. To say I have nothing to pray for shows a lack of faith, ignorance of the Bible, and laziness. Failure to pray is sin! Prayer is not an option. If you are not praying, then you are either backslidden or not saved. We are commanded to pray.

> Be careful for nothing; but in everything by prayer and supplication with thanksgiving let your requests be made known unto God. And the peace of God, which passeth all understanding, shall keep your hearts and minds through Christ Jesus. (Philippians 4:6–7)

We are not to be worried or anxious over our circumstances or weaknesses, but to confess them and give them to The Most High in prayer. We give up so much peace when we keep our problems and the world's problems to ourselves. He says make your request known unto Him. Remember, He knows what we need before we ask Him. But He tells us to pray anyway. You do not make a request to someone unless you think that person can give you the request. Always give thanks to Him, not just when your prayers are answered but in everything. Failing to do this shows a lack of gratitude.

> In everything give thanks; for this is the will of God in Christ Jesus concerning you. (1 Thessalonians 5:18)

Does this mean thanking Him for bringing you through your situations or giving thanks for the situation? It means both. Everything moves by the power of The Most High.

> For in him we live and move and have our being;
> as certain also of your own poets have said, for we
> are his offspring. (Acts 17:28)

> And all the inhabitants of the earth are reputed
> as nothing and he doeth according to his will in
> the army of the earth; and none can stay his hand
> or say unto him What doest thou? (Daniel 4:35)

We must accept the fact that God is sovereign, He is just, and as God of all the earth, He will do right. He does not ask us permission before He allows events to happen. If you read the book of Job, you will see Job was never told why the enemy was allowed to do the things he did unto him. Read the following:

> Moreover the Lord answered Job, and said, Shall
> he that content with the almighty instruct him? He
> that reproveth God, let him answer it, Then Job
> answered the Lord, and said, Behold I am vile; what
> shall I answer thee? I will lay mine hand upon my
> mouth. Once have I spoken but I will not answer:
> ye, twice: but I will proceed no further. (Job 40:1–5)

After Job was given a thorough education of the sovereignty of The Most High, Job realized all he thought he knew was wrong. We are like Job, running on what we think we know because we listen to a preacher or teacher who does not know their subject matter. They teach wrong, and many follow their wrong junk. And the only way to get on the right track is:

> Study to show thyself approved unto God, a
> workman that needeth not to be ashamed, rightly
> dividing the word of truth. (2 Timothy 2:15)

We have a greater advantage than Job. We have the written word of The Most High: the Bible.

> And when he had sent the multitudes away, he went up into a mountain apart to pray: and when the evening was come, he was there alone. (Matthew 14:23)

> And in the morning, rising up a great while before day, he went out, and departed into a solitary place and there prayed. (Mark 1:35)

> And he withdrew himself into the wilderness, and prayed. (Luke 5:16)

> And it came to pass in those days, that he went out into a mountain to pray, and he continued all night in prayer to God. (Luke 6:12)

Jesus not only came to die for our sins but to give us examples in dealing with Himself. He, the most perfect man, the very God, prayed. Therefore, it is a must for us to find time away from others to pray. Find a place and time without distractions. There are many distractions to prayer: TV, computers, cell phones, people, and the things of this world. I like to pray and study in the early morning when all I hear are the birds singing (or are they praying?). I want no questions, no man-made sound. When you first start praying, it will be hard. Your flesh and the enemy will find all kinds of excuses for you not to pray (Matthew 13:18–23).

> And he cometh and findeth them sleeping, saith unto Peter, Simon, sleepest thou? Could not thou watch one hour? Watch ye and pray lest ye enter into temptation. The spirit truly is ready, but the flesh is weak. (Mark 14:37–38)

The flesh is the weak link between us and The Most High. Your flesh will find all kinds of reasons not to pray. Thus, you must find all kinds of reasons to pray (Romans 7:13–25).

Worship must always be part of your prayers. In the model prayer, Jesus taught us to worship.

> After this manner therefore pray ye: Our Father which art in heaven Hallowed be thy name. (Matthew 6:9)

Notice the prayer is opened with worship. I do not mean flowering words such as the great omnipotent one. Yes, He is all powerful, and He knows that. He also knows when you are trying to do a flattering job on Him. In Acts 4:23–32, 16:25, the people worshipped as they prayed. Worship is part of prayer.

WHAT DO WE PRAY FOR?

> After this manner therefore pray ye: Our Father
> which art in heaven, hallowed be thy name. Thy
> kingdom come. Thy will be done in earth, as it is
> in heaven. Give us this day our daily bread. And
> forgive us our debts, as we forgive our debtors,
> And lead us not into temptation, but deliver us
> from evil; For thine is the kingdom and the power
> and the glory, forever. Amen. (Matthew 6:9–13)

This is a model prayer; notice that Jesus said, "Pray after this manner." This is to be a guide as you begin to learn to pray. This should not be your prayer word for word every day. In our prayers, we are to honor The Most High, pray His kingdom come, His will be done on earth, thank Him for our daily sustenance, to be kept from temptation and evil, and pray for our sins to be forgiven as we forgive others their sins against us. Your closure should be giving Him honor and glory.

The following is for husbands.

> Likewise, ye husbands, dwell with them accord-
> ing to knowledge, giving honor unto the wife,
> as unto the weaker vessel, and as being heirs
> together of the grace of life; That your prayers be
> not hindered. (1 Peter 3:7)

Men, anger with your wife hinders your prayers from being heard on high.

> Watch and pray that ye enter not into temptation: the spirit indeed is willing, but the flesh is weak. He went away again the second time, and prayed, saying, O my Father, if this cup may not pass away from me, except I drink it, thy will be done. (Matthew 26:41–42)

> And the Lord said, Simon, Simon, behold, Satan have desire to have ye that he may shift you as wheat but I have prayed for you that thy faith fail not and when thou art converted strengthen thy brethren. (Luke 22:31–32)

> But when he saw the multitudes, he was moved with compassion on them, because they fainted, and were scattered abroad, as sheep having no shepherd. Then said he unto his disciples, the harvest truly is plenteous, but the laborers are few; Pray ye therefore the lord of the harvest, that he would send forth laborers into his harvest. (Matthew 9:36–38)

> But I say unto you, love your enemies, bless them that curse you, do good to them that hate you, and pray for them which despite fully use you, and persecute you; That you may be the children of your Father which is in heaven: for he maketh his sun to rise on the evil and on the good, and sendeth rain on the just and on the unjust. (Matthew 5:44–45)

Jesus is telling us not to get weary in prayer. We are always to be vigilant in prayer. Pray for yourselves and others to be ready to stand in the time of trials and temptation. Pray for more people to be soul winners. Pray for those who are against you or other saints.

We are to pray for the peace of Jerusalem.

> Pray for the peace of Jerusalem, they shall prosper
> that love thee. (Psalm 122:6)

The Jews are still the first nation of The Most High. Christians have not replaced them. Please read the following verses on your own: Jeremiah 31:34–37, 33:20–21, 25–26. And you must read Romans chapter 11. Listen, to hate Israel is to hate yourself because you will be cursed.

> And I will bless them that bless thee, and curse
> him that curseth thee: and in thee shall all fami-
> lies of the earth be blessed. (Genesis 12:3)

Israel is not right in everything it does, but it is still the first nation of The Most High. And if you wish to prosper, you must love and pray for Israel. And remember, Jesus Christ was born a Jew.

WORLDLINESS

Worldliness is a great hindrance to steadfast prayer. This is a vast topic, so I am not going to cover all it entails. Talk to your pastor about it. Look at these:

> No man that warreth entangleth himself with the affairs of this life; that he may please him who hath chosen him to be a soldier. (2 Timothy 2:4)

> Stand fast therefore in the liberty wherewith Christ hath made us free, and be not entangled again with the yoke of bondage. (Galatians 5:1)

How far does the word *entanglement* go? *Strong's Exhaustive Concordance* tells us that *entanglement* means not to be twisted up in the world's affairs.

> Ye ask, and receive not, because you asked a miss, that you may consume it upon your lust. You adulterers and adulteresses, know you not that the friendship of the world is enmity with God? Whosoever therefore will be friend of the world is the enemy of God. (James 4:3–4)

If you call yourself a friend of this world, you are an enemy of God. We know we must work and live in this system. But we are not to be of the world but in the world. Let me explain: your fingers and thumbs on your hands are made into your hands. But if you place your keys in your hand, they are not of your hand but have been placed into your hand. Thus, once we are saved, we are no longer *of* this world, but we live temporarily *in* this world until we are taken to heaven (John 17:10–21).

> I wrote unto you in an epistle not to company with fornicators: Yet not altogether with the fornicators of this world, or with the covetous, or extortioners, or with idolaters; for then must ye needs go out of the world. But now I have written unto you not to keep company, if any man that is called a brother be a fornicator or covetous, or an idolater, or a railer, or a drunkard, or an extortioner; with such a one, no, not to eat. (1 Corinthians 5:9–11)

We must live, work, and shop in this sinful world, but we must live differently. To get away from all the evil in this world, we would have to be taken out of this world. We must not allow ourselves to become tainted or influenced by the sins of this world.

> Be ye not unequally yoked together with unbelievers: for what fellowship hath righteousness with unrighteousness? And what communion hath light with darkness? And what concord hath Christ with Belial? Or what part hath he that believeth with an infidel? And what agreement hath the temple of God with idols? For ye are the temple of the living God; as God hath said, I will dwell in them, and walk in them and I will be their God, and they shall be my people. Wherefore come out from among them and be ye separate, saith the Lord, and touch not the unclean thing: and I will receive you, and

will be a Father unto you, and ye shall be my sons and daughters, saith the Lord Almighty. (2 Corinthians 6:14–18)

We must be careful to ensure any time we have to interact with nonbelievers, we must not allow ourselves to be tainted with their beliefs and actions.

And these are they which are sown among thorns; such as hear the word, and the cares of this world, and the deceitfulness of riches, and the lust of other things entering in, choke the word and it becometh unfruitful. (Mark 4:18–19)

Entanglement with the world or worldliness will choke the word of The Most High and prayer right out of you. And you will become unfruitful. Let us take a little test. Would you rather talk about politics or the Bible? Men, do you know more about golf, football, or baseball than you know about the book of Romans? Ladies, do you know more about soap operas and dresses than you know about the book of St. John? Both men and women, can you tell someone why you are going to heaven? Would you rather look at the TV or read and study your Bible? Are you *in* the world or *of* the world (John 17)?

And take heed to yourselves, lest at any time your hearts be overcharged with surfeiting (over-eating), and drunkenness, and cares of this life, and so that day come upon you unawares. For as a snare shall it come on all them that dwell on the face of the whole earth. Watch ye therefore, and pray always, that ye may be accounted worthy to escape all these things that shall come to pass, and to stand before the Son of man. (Luke 21:34–36)

Man, this is some serious stuff.

We are to pray before we enter into temptations, be it overeating, party lifestyle, or just failure to see the end-times we are living in. We are not to be like the world; we are children of the day (God), not children of the night (satan).

> And said (Jesus) unto them; Why sleep ye? Rise and pray, lest ye enter into temptation. (Luke 22:46)

We are also to watch and pray that we be counted worthy to escape what is to come upon the earth in these last days.

> Watch ye therefore, and pray always, that ye may be accounted worthy to escape all these things that shall come to pass, and to stand before the Son of man. (Luke 21:36)

EXHORTATION TO PRAY

I exhort therefore, that, first of all, supplications, prayers, intercessions, and giving of thanks, be made for all men. For kings and for all that are in authority; that we may lead a quiet and peaceable life in all godliness and honesty. For this is good and acceptable in the sight of God our Savior; Who will have all men to be saved and to come unto the knowledge of the truth. For there is one God, and one mediator between God and men, the man Christ Jesus; Who gave himself a ransom for all, to be testified in due time. Whereunto I am ordained a preacher, and an apostle, (I speak the truth in Christ, and lie not:) a teacher of the Gentiles in faith and verity I will therefore that men pray everywhere, lifting up holy hands, without wrath and doubting. In like manner also that women adorn themselves in modest apparel, with shamefacedness and sobriety; not with braided hair, or gold or pearls, or costly array; But (which becometh women professing godliness) with good works. (1 Timothy 2:1–9)

This is similar to verses found in Jeremiah. The Most High gave this unto the Jews when they were taken captive to Babylon. This is found in Jeremiah 29:4–9, but I am giving you verse 7: "And seek the peace of the city whither I have caused you to be carried away captives, and pray unto the Lord for it: for in the peace thereof shall ye have peace."

We should pray, intercede, and give thanks for all men—government leaders (both domestic and foreign, good and bad), pastors, policemen, firemen, tax collectors, judges, school leaders, your neighbors, and others. This includes all church leaders.

The Most High's will is for all people to be saved and understand Him and His Christ. Pray for them to be convicted of sin, righteousness, and judgement by The Holy Spirit. Those who believe some people are destined to be saved and some are destined to hell are wrong; this verse puts that notion to rest. The Most High's will is for all mankind to be saved.

We are to pray lifting holy hands, which means we are to confess our sins before we pray. And we should come in full assurance that He hears our prayers. If you have wrath, get rid of it. It does not matter how terribly you were treated; you cannot come before Him with wrath and rage. Unless you are praying to get rid of it.

> Wherefore my beloved brethren, let every man
> be swift to hear, slow to speak, slow to wrath: For
> the wrath of man worketh not the righteousness
> of God. (James 1:19–20)

If you have doubt, then pray for Him to help you with your unbelief. "Help thou mine unbelief" (Mark 9:24).

Ladies, you are to pray in like manner of holiness. You must not be so concerned about the latest style, hairdo, or how good a figure you have or don't have. The Most High puts this in His Bible because He knows the world influences women more than men when it comes to dress and appearance. Remember this: there will be some beautiful women and handsome men in hell.

HEAD COVERING FOR WOMEN

This is a controversial subject. I hope I do not make it any worse. Should women pray with a cloth on their heads? This is found in:

> But every woman that prayeth or prophesieth with her head uncovered dishonoreth her head; for that is even all one as if she were shaven. For if the woman be not covered, let her also be shorn: but if it be a shame for a woman to be shorn or shaven, let her be covered. (1 Corinthians 11:5–6)

I am not about to take a deep dive into this subject but a little jump.

> But if a woman have long hair, it is a glory to her: for her hair is given her for a covering. But if any man seem to be contentious, we have no such custom, neither the churches of God. (1 Corinthians 11:15–16)

Women, your hair is given to you as your covering. Nothing in the scriptures says how long or short it is to be. And from reading verse 16, it says, "We have no such custom in the churches of God." That tells me The Lord was talking about some pagan practice of shaving women's hair before they worship an idol. We do not worship idols; we worship The Most High, and the only requirement is:

> But the hour cometh, and now is when the true worshipers shall worship the Father in spirit and in truth: for the Father seeketh such to worship him. (John 4:23)

Ladies, you do not need a head covering to come to church, to take communion, or to pray in church.

Are you sick? Pray.

> Is any among you afflicted? Let him pray. (James 5:13)

Leave the healing to The Most High. It is up to Him to give you healing, not your righteousness or your sinfulness.

Let us move on.

> Praying always with all prayer and supplication in the spirit. And watching therefore unto all perseverance and supplication for all saints: and for me that utterance may be given unto me that I may open my mouth boldly, to make known the mysteries of the gospel. (Ephesians 6:18–19)

When was the last time you prayed for Christian workers or your pastor to be given the right words in spreading the gospel? What about other saints? Do you pray for your fellow saints? Do you follow-up your prayers with action?

> If a brother or sister be naked, and destitute of daily food. And one of you say unto them, depart in peace, be warm and filled; Notwithstanding ye give them not those things which are needful to the body; What does it profit? Even so faith, if it hath not works, is dead, being alone. (James 2:15–17)

> If any of you lack wisdom, let him ask of God, that giveth to all men liberally, and upbraideth not and it shall be given him. But let him ask in faith, nothing wavering. For he that wavereth is like a wave of the sea driven with the wind and

tossed. For let not that man think he shall receive
anything of the Lord. A double-minded man, is
unstable in all his ways. (James 1:5–7)

Ask for wisdom; do not waver in your prayers. Be steadfast and
unmovable when you pray. Pray that you do not do stupid things
that could hurt your witness, your family, or yourself.

Trust in the Lord with all thine heart; and lean
not unto thine own understanding. In all thy
ways acknowledge him, and he shall direct thy
paths. (Proverbs 3:5–6)

Pray for guidance in all that you do, especially big decisions. But
ensure your answer is from The Most High and not some prophet or
prophetess.

And her prophets have daubed them with untam-
pered mortar (not true words), seeing vanity,
and divining lies unto them saying, Thus saith
the Lord God, when the Lord hath not spoken.
(Ezekiel 22:28)

Also read Ezekiel 13:6–8.

Wannabe spiritual leaders will tell you that The Lord told them
to tell you to do something, go somewhere, or even give them your
money. Be careful in this area. I have met saints who have ruined
their lives and that of their family because they listen to one of these
charlatans. I get those spiritual folks telling me what The Most High
has told them to tell me. And I reply to them, "I pray to Him every
day, and He has not told me anything like that." Now He may use
someone else to confirm what He has already told me, but I am still
careful.

I thank my God upon every remembrance of you.
Always in every prayer of mine for you all mak-

ing a request with joy, for your fellowship in the
gospel from the first day until now. (Philippians
1:3–5)

Are you praying with joy for others and for fellowship to
flourish?

Did you know failure to pray for someone is sin?

Moreover as for me, God forbid that I should sin
against the Lord in ceasing to pray for you. (1
Samuel 12:23)

When others ask you to pray for them, do so right then if possible. You might be the person The Most High sent to pray for them.
There are certain people our Father desires to pray for others. Never
be afraid to tell someone what is wrong with you; he or she could
be the person The Most High has sent to pray for you. You are not
looking for their sympathy but their prayers.

You also should pray for others as they are brought to your
mind. Let me issue a caution here: know who labors among you.
Be careful who you allow to pray for you. You do not want a person
who does not believe to pray for you. The Most High will not send
an unsaved person to pray for you because He does not hear their
prayers until they want salvation.

If I regard iniquity in my heart, the Lord will not
hear me. (Psalm 66:18)

Now we know that God heareth not sinners: but
if any man be a worshiper of God, and do his
will, him he heareth. (John 9:31)

Notice what happened to Job after he prayed for his friends.

And it was so, that after the Lord had spoken
these words unto Job, the Lord said to Eliphaz the

Temanite, "My wrath is kindled against thee, and against thy two friends: for ye have not spoken of me the thing that is right, as my servant Job hath. Therefore, take to you now seven bullocks and seven rams, and go to my servant Job, and offer up for yourselves a burnt offering; and my servant Job shall pray for you: for him will I accept lest I deal with you after your folly, in that you have not spoken of me the thing that is right, like my servant Job." So, Eliphaz the Temanite and Bildad the Shuhite and Zophar the Naamathite went and did according as the Lord commanded them: the Lord also accepted Job. And the Lord turned the captivity of Job, when he prayed for his friends: also, the Lord gave Job twice as much as he had before. (Job 42:7–10)

Notice that The Lord did not restore anything to Job until he prayed for his three friends. Job said some harsh things about The Most High. But Job repented (Job 42:6), and it was as if he had never uttered those words. After Job got right with The Most High, he prayed for his friends, thus becoming an intercessor or daysman (mediator) (Job 9:33) for them.

Is any among you afflicted? Let him pray, is any merry? Let him sing Psalms. Is any sick among you? Let him call for the elders of the church; and let them pray over him, anointing him with oil in the name of the Lord: And the prayer of faith shall save the sick, and the Lord shall raise him up; and if he have committed sins, they shall be forgiven him. Confess your faults one to another, pray one for another, that ye may be healed. The effectual fervent prayer of a righteous man availeth much, Elijah was a man subject to like passions as we are and he prayed earnestly that it

might not rain: and it rained not on the earth by
the space of three years and six months. And he
prayed again and the heaven gave rain, and the
earth brought forth her fruit. (James 5:13–18)

When you have prayed for yourselves and you do not receive
your answer. Then you should call for the elders of the church.
Whether it is an elder or a regular person, that person should be an
unceasing, fervent, and earnest prayer person. The Lord told Elijah
that at Elijah's word, the rain would stop and the rain would come
again. Elijah prayed seven times before the rain started again (1 King
17:1, 18:41–46).

A holy anointing oil was used in the Old Testament temple. It
was not to be used on anyone but the high priest and the furnish-
ing in the temple (Exodus 30:22–38). Regular olive oil was used to
anoint kings. In the New Testament, it was used as follows:

And they cast out many devils, and anointed
with oil many that were sick, and healed them.
(Mark 6:13)

We are called to pray for people. I do not know what the oil
symbolizes. Was it the oil or faith that brought the healing? The Bible
says use it, so use it if The Lord leads you. We do not have holy water
or oil. Both of those are used in conjunction with temple worship.
A co-worker once brought me a small vial of water taken from the
River Jordan. He thought he was doing something great. I thanked
him and went on my way. The water did not look any different than
water here in the USA. It has no special properties. It was not holy.
So be careful about using these so-called holy items. You do not need
to buy oil that someone has labeled as holy. Just use a little cooking
oil or olive oil on a finger. No need to drown someone in oil.

The oil is not to be used as a magic potion. It says nothing
about putting it on your walls or some other object; it is to be used
on people for healing. And nowhere in scripture is oil used to cast out

demons or to keep demons away. Notice "confess your faults one to another." When you offend someone, get it right quickly, if possible.

> And Jesus answering saith unto them. Have faith in God. For verily I say unto you, that whosoever shall say unto this mountain, be thou removed, and be thou cast into the sea; And shall not doubt in his heart but shall believe that those things which he say shall come to pass; He shall have whatsoever he said. Therefore, I say unto you, what things soever you desire, when you pray, believe that you receive them, and you shall have them. And when you stand praying, forgive if you have aught against any: that your Father which also is in heaven may forgive you your trespasses. But if you do not forgive, neither will your father, which is in heaven forgive your trespasses. (Mark 11:22–26)

As you can see from reading the above text, you must have faith in God to not only save you but to hear and answer your prayers. Plus, you must not hold unforgiveness against anyone. If you do not forgive, He will not forgive you. Check your life for any hint of unforgiveness. Do you hold something against a spouse, relative, friend, or stranger? Do you get upset thinking about some incidents from your past that were against you? Did someone misuse your trust? Did someone steal from you or hurt you in actions or words? You must pray about it, give it to The Most High, and let Him take care of it.

> Looking diligently lest any man fail of the grace of God; lest any root of bitterness springing up trouble you, and thereby many be defiled. (Hebrews 12:15)

I had a root of bitterness growing in me, and I had to let The Most High kill it. I began to hate the people who were responsible for shooting me in 2010. (Read the book *On Point!: The Making of a Prison Contraband Captain*.) I had to let The Most High kill that root and other roots of bitterness. Bitterness has the potential to destroy many. In a church, bitterness over picking a pastor, the color of carpet, or the choice of an organ can spread from one person to a group of people and defile the whole church. Look deep and let Him do His work. We are imperfect people in an imperfect world. Only Christ lived a perfect life. Therefore, we must live our lives through Him by walking in the Spirit. We must depend on Him; our flesh is very weak.

NAME IT AND CLAIM IT

There is a doctrine called "name it and claim it," which has created a number of liars. This doctrine teaches that all you must do is name what you want and claim it, believe for it, and receive it in Jesus's name. There was an extremely popular song with that title in it. You cannot demand what you want from The Most High. Try to demand something from the president of the United States and see what you get. You do not have the right to claim anything other than your salvation and help in the time of trouble.

I have met believers who are sick and when asked, "How are you doing?" they lie and say, "I am healed," when in fact they are still sick. This lie is called "positive confession, name it and claim it, or divine health." Any positive confession must line up with His will. The correct answer should be, "I am still believing for my healing; I believe The Most High. He is sovereign and will always do what is right." Anything more is a presumptuous lie and is not an indicator of faith.

There is nothing in scripture that says we will not be sick, have body ailments, or even die. I know many preachers teach this, but it does not line up with scripture. They may not speak it, but Arthur

(Arthritis) will get all of them. Sooner or later, they will all die of something. There is a web site called Born of Spirit. I would not advise anyone to visit that site. Scriptures are twisted to get what the author wants them to say.

> (As it is written, I have made thee a father of many nations,) before him whom he believed, even God, who quickeneth the dead, and calleth those things which be not as though they were. (Romans 4:17)

I have heard many saints take this verse out of context. It tells us only God can give life to that which was dead. Only He can speak those things that have not happened as though they are already in existence.

The Most High is sovereign and has not given any of us the right to tell him what we demand. You cannot decree or declare anything other than your willingness to let Him be ruler of everything. There is no scripture to support decreeing or declaring. Sounds good, but not biblical.

PUBLIC VERSUS PRIVATE PRAYER

· · · ·

> When thou prayest, thou should not be as the hypocrite are: for they love to pray standing in the synagogues and in the corners of the streets, that they may be seen of men. Verily I say unto you, they have their reward. But thou, when thou prayest, enter into thy closet, and when thou has shut thy door, pray to thy Father which is in secret; And thy Father which seeth in secret shall reward thee openly, but when you pray, use not vain repetitions, as the heathens do: for they think that they shall be heard for their much

speaking. Be not ye therefore like unto them for
your Father know what things you have need of,
before you ask him. (Matthew 6:5–7)

Our Savior has given us a lot to digest. When in public, we are not to pray to impress others with our command of the English language, nor to be seen by others. To do so will give you an earthly reward, the admiration of others. Earthly admiration will do nothing in getting your prayers heard or answered. When in public, do not pray long prayers (Mark 12:38–40), unless the Holy Spirit is really prompting you. Do not use vain (fillers), repetitive empty, meaningless words. The Most High knows who He is and His own capabilities. Screaming is not needed; He knows who we are, and His hearing is exceptionally good.

You do not need to tell Him to go to the nursing home or hospital. You go there and pray for them. We cannot stroke our Father's ego with fancy names. Get to the point. Pray your longest prayers in secret, and our Father, who hears in secret, will reward you openly. Do not use your prayers to counsel those who are listening. Be careful when using His name; He knows you are praying to Him, so there is no need to keep using His name over and over. I am not saying we should not use His name, but do not let it become a filler (more on this later).

In a public prayer meeting, do not set a time length for each person's prayer. Let them say what they have to say and then move on to the next person. This is especially true for pastors or prayer leaders. Do not tell someone, "I want you to pray for thirty minutes." That person may not be that far along in their prayer life, and all you will get is fillers. I have stopped accepting invitations to functions and events just to pray. This is just a tradition and could be considered a performance for men. As I said earlier, I cringe when people say what a great prayer I prayed. I know they mean well, but my prayer was for our Father's approval and not for theirs.

Your longest prayer should be in private, just The Most High and you. We have showboaters who love to pray long oratorical Shakespearean prayers in public and will not pray in private. As I said before, you do not need to use thou, thy, thither, thee, or beholdest. Pray using regular English. There is no such thing as a public prayer ministry. The Most High cannot be fooled by us. Those of you who like to pray those long prayers, examine yourselves and see why you really pray that way. If The Most High is leading you to pray a long prayer, then pray as He leads.

CURSING OR BLESSING

. . . .

> Bless them that curse you and pray for them which despitefully use you. (Luke 6:28)

> Bless them which persecute you: bless, and curse not. (Romans 12:14)

No prayer should ever be used to curse or come against any human being; instead, we are to pray for them to be blessed, and if they are not saved, pray for them to be saved. Remember, the wrath of man does not work the righteousness of The Most High (James 1:20). Pray against the evil spirit that is influencing them to do evil against you.

Remember, Jesus said:

> Then said Jesus, Father, forgive them; For they know not what they do. (Luke 23:34)

Stephen also:

> And he kneeled down, and cried with a loud voice, Lord lay not this sin to their charge. And when he had said this, he fell asleep. (Acts 7:60)

Use fervent prayer to bless those who persecute or attack you.

Prayers, when possible, should be spoken. Let me show you why.

> My voice shall thou hear in the morning, O Lord;
> in the morning will I direct my prayers unto thee
> and will look up. (Psalm 5:3)

> Death and life are in the power of the tongue:
> and they that love it shall eat the fruit thereof.
> (Proverbs 18:21)

> As for me, I will call upon God; And the Lord
> will save me. Evening, and morning, and at
> noon, will I pray and cry aloud: and he shall hear
> my voice. (Psalm 55:16–17)

> Let the words of my mouth, and the meditation
> of my heart, be acceptable in thy sight, O Lord,
> my strength, and my Redeemer. (Psalm 19:14)

Yes, He can read our minds, but our prayers should be spoken if possible. There is a song entitled "Silent Prayer Request." It is a good-sounding song, but not a song based on scripture.

> Take with you words and turn to The Lord.
> (Hosea 14:2)

> Then said he unto me, Fear not, Daniel: for
> from the first day that thou didst set thine heart
> to understand, and to chasten thyself before thy
> God, thy words were heard, and I am come for
> thy words. (Daniel 10:12)

> And Samuel grew, and the Lord was with him,
> and did not let none of his words fall to the
> ground. (1 Samuel 3:19)

O generation of Vipers, how can ye, being evil, speak good things? Out of the abundance of the heart (mind) the mouth speaketh. A good man out of the good treasure of the heart bringeth forth good things: and an evil man out of the evil treasure bringeth forth evil things. But I say unto you, that every idle word that men shall speak, they shall give an account thereof in the day of judgment. For by thy words, thou shalt be justified, and by thy words thou shalt be condemned. (Matthew 12:34–37)

But what saith it? The word is nigh thee, even in thy mouth and in thy heart: that is the Word of Faith, which we preach; That if thou confess with thy mouth the Lord Jesus, and shalt believe in thine heart that God hath raised him from the dead, thou shall be saved. For with the heart man believeth unto righteousness and with the mouth confession is made unto salvation. (Romans 10:8–10)

Our words are powerful; an illegal use of words can actually kill. You can speak evil words into certain people's lives, and they can be influenced to kill themselves. You can also influence them by speaking good, encouraging words. Pray for your mind to be filled with love for others, and that is what will come out of your mouth.

There was a certain man in Caesarea called Cornelius, a centurion of the band called the Italian band, a devout man, one that feared God with all his house, which gave much alms to the people; and prayed to God always. He saw in a vision evidently about the ninth hour of the day an angel of God coming into him, and saying unto him Cornelius. And when he looked on him, he was afraid, and said, what is it, Lord? And he said unto him, thy prayers and thy alms are come up for a memorial before God. (Acts 10:1–4)

Cornelius righteous spoken prayers went up to The Most High. Cornelius's prayers were recorded and kept (memorial) by The Most High. Our righteous spoken prayers are collected in heaven and will be used to bring future judgments upon the earth. Our prayers rise like incense to Him.

Ye shall offer no strange incense thereon, nor burnt sacrifice, nor meat offering: neither shall ye pour drink offering thereon. (Exodus 30:9)

And he shall take a censer full of burning coals of fire from off the altar before the Lord, and his hands full of sweet incense beaten small, and bring it within the veil: And he shall put the incense upon the fire before the Lord, that the cloud of the incense may cover the mercy seat that is upon the testimony, that he die not. (Leviticus 16:12–13)

Let my prayer be set forth before thee as incense; and the lifting up of my hands as the evening sacrifice. (Psalm 141:2)

And when he had taken the book, the four beasts and the four and twenty elders fell down before the lamb, having every one of them harps, and golden vials full of odors (incense) which are the prayers of Saints. (Revelation 5:8)

And when he had opened the seventh seal, there was silence in heaven about the space of half an hour. And I saw the seven angels which stood before God; and to them were given seven trumpets. And another Angel came out and stood at the altar, having a golden censor; And there was given unto him much incense, that he should offer it with the prayers of all saints upon the golden altar which was before the throne. And the smoke of the incense which came with the prayers of the saints, ascended up before God out of the angel's hand. And the angel took the censor, and filled it with fire of the altar, and cast it onto the earth: and there were voices, and thundering, and lightning, and an earthquake. (Revelation 8:1–5)

Notice, "there were voices." Are these voices of saints that have prayed throughout the centuries? Yes! Our prayers will be used to help bring judgment upon the earth during the great tribulation.

When you have a prayer request, make it known. Do not keep it to yourself. The Most High has assigned someone to pray for you. Yes, you must be careful not to ask nor allow anyone and everyone to pray for you. But walk in the Spirit, and the Spirit will let you know who to ask for prayer.

I have talked to people who believed if satan hears your prayers, he can stop the answer. That would indicate that satan is more powerful than The Most High. Do not fear him hearing your prayers.

Ye are of God, little children, and have overcome them: because greater is he that's in you, than he that's in the world. (1 John 4:4)

INTERCESSION

Intercessional prayers are for living people. Once someone has died in an unsaved state, they cannot be saved (Hebrews 9:27–28). We pray for living people, they may be sick, or judgement from The Most High may be about to fall on them. You are interceding in an attempt to change Our Father's mind about their situation. I know great preachers say you cannot change His mind, but I beg to differ (more on this later). Why pray if your prayers cannot influence Him according to His will? He introduced the term intercession. So it must be His will. Why would The Most High place it in His Bible if it did not work? This gives me great comfort knowing it is His will for me to intercede on behalf of ourselves or others. And always remember, The Most High will always do that which is right for us.

> Who is he that condemneth? It is Christ that died, yea rather, that is risen again, who is even at the right hand of God, who also maketh intercession for us. (Romans 8:34)

> Therefore he is able also to save them to the uttermost that come unto God by him, seeing he ever liveth, to make intercession for them. (Hebrews 7:25)

Jesus paid the price to become our intercessor by His holy life and painful death on the cross. Jesus is the only intercessor in heaven between us and The Most High. Mary is not, and cannot, intercede for us as the Catholics teach, nor can any dead saint intercede for us. We who are alive are to help in this interceding when we pray for others. We pray for them that they be saved, healed, protected, His will be done in their lives, and for them not to be subject to His wrath. Read the following:

> And I sought for a man among them, that should make up the hedge, and stand in the gap before me for the land, that I should not destroy it: but I found none. Therefore, have I poured out my indignation upon them; I have consumed them with the fire of my wrath: their own way have I recompensed upon their heads saith the Lord. (Ezekiel 22:30–31)

His will is for us to step forward and become earthly intercessors (daymen) on behalf of others.

> And the Lord repented of the evil which he thought to do unto his people. (Exodus 32:14)

> And I fell down before the Lord, as at the first, forty days and forty nights: I didn't either eat bread, or drink water, because of all your sins which ye had sinned, in doing wickedly in the sight of the Lord, to provoke him to anger. For I was afraid of the anger and hot displeasure, wherewith the Lord was wroth against you to destroy you, but the Lord hearkened unto me at that time also and the Lord was very angry with Aaron to have destroyed him: but I prayed for Aaron also the same time. (Deuteronomy 9:18–20)

Therefore he said that he would destroy them, had not Moses his chosen stood before him in the breach, to turn away his wrath, least he should destroy them. (Psalm 106:23)

Moses interceded for Israel multiple times. If he had not, the whole nation would have been destroyed (Exodus 32:9–11).

Read Genesis chapters 18 and 19. The Most High stopped by Abraham's tent on His way to destroy all the cities of the plain to include Sodom and Gomorrah because their sin (homosexuality) was great and very grievous (18:20) to Him. His mind was made up to destroy that area, but Abraham knew Lot lived in Sodom. Abraham began to intercede on behalf of the cities of that area. Abraham interceded five times with The Most High. From fifty down to ten righteous people, and those cities would not have been destroyed. But ten could not be found, but read the following:

And it came to pass, when God destroyed the cities of the plain, that God remembered Abraham, and sent Lot out of the midst of the overthrow, when he overthrew the cities in the which Lot dwelt. (Genesis 19:29)

Can you believe that, even though the bargain was not met, The Most High showed Lot mercy because He did not want to cause Abraham grief at the loss of Lot. Don't tell me our Father is not merciful.

In those days was Hezekiah sick unto death. And the prophet Isaiah the son of Amoz came to him, and said unto him, thus saith the Lord, set thy house in order for thou shalt die and not live. Then he turned his face to the wall, and prayed unto the Lord, saying I beseech thee, oh Lord, remember now how I have walked before thee in truth and with a perfect heart, and have done

that which is good in thy sight. And Hezekiah
wept sore. And it came to pass afore Isaiah was
gone out of the middle court that the word of the
Lord came to him, saying, Turn again and tell
Hezekiah the captain of my people, thus saith the
Lord the God of David thy father I have heard
thy prayer I have seen thy tears behold I will heal
thee: On the third day thou shalt go up into the
House of the Lord. (2 Kings 20:1–5)

King Hezekiah interceded for himself and was given fifteen
more years. If The Most High did not change His mind, what did
He do? This does not take away from His omniscience (all-knowing).
Because He is The Most High, He is Sovereign and He always does
what is right. Knowing this gives me assurance that He will hear my
intercession for myself and others. He changes His mind because of
our prayers. His will is still being done because we prayed. So always
remember that He put intercessions in place.

Whereupon the princes of Israel and the king
humbled themselves; and they said, The Lord
is righteous And when the Lord saw that they
humbled themselves, the word of the Lord came
to Shemaiah, saying, they have humbled themselves; therefore, I will not destroy them, but I
will grant them some deliverance; and my wrath
shall not be poured out upon Jerusalem by the
hand of Shishak. (2 Chronicles 12:6–7)

Never let anyone tell you that The Most High's mind cannot be
changed sometimes by our actions. Remember 2 Chronicles 7:13–14.

But there was none like unto Ahab, which did
sell himself to work wickedness in the sight of the
Lord, whom Jezebel his wife stirred up. And he
did very abominable in following idols, accord-

ing to all things as did the Amorites, whom the Lord cast out before the children of Israel. And it came to pass, when Ahab heard those words, that he rent his clothes, and put sackcloth upon his flesh, and fasted, and lay in sackcloth, and went softly. And the word of the Lord came to Elijah the Tishbite, saying, Seest thou how Ahab humbleth himself before me? Because he humbleth himself before me, I will not bring the evil in his days: but in his son's days will I bring the evil upon his house. (1 Kings 21:25–29)

Elijah told King Ahab that The Most High was going to bring much evil upon Ahab's house. But Ahab humbled himself. Notice humbleness. The Most High hates pride.

Jesus interceded for Peter and us.

And the Lord said, Simon, Simon, behold, Satan hath desired to have you, that he may shift you as wheat: but I have prayed for you that thy faith fail not: and when thou art converted, strengthen thy brethren. (Luke 22:31–32)

Neither pray I for these alone, but for them also which shall believe on me through their word. (John 17:20)

The Spirit also intercedes for us.

Likewise the Spirit also helpeth our infirmities: for we know not what we should pray for as we ought: but the Spirit itself maketh intercession for us with groanings which cannot be uttered. And he that searched the hearts knoweth what is in the mind of the Spirit, because he maketh intercession for the Saints according to the will of

> God. And we know that all things work together
> for good to them that love God, to them who
> are the called according to his purpose. (Romans
> 8:26–28)

The Holy Spirit knows what is in the mind of The Most High; therefore, he knows how to make perfect intercession for us.

In the book of Acts, chapter 12, James and Peter were placed in prison by King Herod.

> And He (Herod the King) killed James the
> brother of John with the sword. (Acts 12:2)

> Peter therefore was kept in prison: but prayer was
> made without ceasing of the church unto God
> for him. (Acts 12:5)

James was killed, but an angel set Peter free (verses 6–10). One was killed, the other set free. Why? The will of The Most High was done. Was prayer made for James? I am sure it was, but it was The Father's will for James to die. What would have happened had the saints not conducted spiritual warfare (prayed) for Peter? I do not know. But I do know that an intercessory prayer was made to The Most High for Peter's freedom. We may think this is cruel and uncaring to let James die, but who are we to find fault with The Most High (Romans 9:10–20)?

There are times the Holy Spirit presses upon us to pray for others, and we may not know their name or what they need. For me, it is like pressure within my body, which is relieved when I pray. I pray as He gives me the words. This is not praying in tongues, but praying as The Holy Spirit prompts you. The Most High also tells us that all things work together for good to those who love God. We know all things that happen to us are not good, but He takes those things that happen to us who love Him and works them for good according to His will. You may not agree with the results, but rest assured it is for our good, and He is righteous. We must learn to forgo many of our earthly desires and see things in His heavenly and righteous will.

HIS WILL BE DONE

· · · · ·

And when he was come unto us, he took Paul's girdle and bound his own hands and feet, and saith, thus said the Holy Ghost, so shall the Jews at Jerusalem bind the man that owneth this girdle and shall deliver him into the hands of the Gentiles. And when we heard these things both we and they of that place, besought him not to go up to Jerusalem. Then Paul answered. What mean ye to weep and to break mine heart? For I am ready not to be bound only but also to die at Jerusalem for the name of the Lord Jesus. And when he would not be persuaded, we ceased, saying the will of the Lord be done. (Acts 21:11–14)

His will is to be done. When you perceive that His will has been done, then and only then you may stop praying for that issue. You may pray for an issue for years. I have heard people say, "Once you pray for something, do not pray for it again. To do so shows a lack of faith." That is an incorrect statement. Here is why:

And he cometh up to his disciples, and find them asleep and said unto Peter what, could you not watch with me one hour? Watch and pray, that you enter not into temptation: the spirit indeed is willing, but the flesh is weak. He went away again the second time, and prayed, saying, O my Father, if this cup may not pass away from me, except I drink it, thy will be done and he came and found them asleep: for their eyes were heavy.

And he left them, and went away again and prayed the third time, saying the same words. (Matthew 26:40–44)

Jesus is giving us an example; He prayed the exact same words three times. Even though Jesus knew His Father's will. He still prayed.

And Lest I should be exalted above measure through the abundance of the revelation, there was given to me a thorn in the flesh, the messenger of Satan to buffet me, least I should be exalted above measure. For this thing I've besought the Lord thrice that it might depart from me. And he said unto me, my grace is sufficient for thee: for my strength is made perfect in weakness. Most gladly therefore will I glory in my infirmities, that the power of Christ may rest upon me. Therefore, I take pleasure in infirmities, in reproaches, in necessities, in persecutions, in distresses for Christ's sake: for when I am weak then am I strong. (2 Corinthians 12:7–10)

I thank my God upon every remembrance of you, always in every prayer of mine for you all making requests with joy. (Philippians 1:3–4)

We give thanks to God and the Father of our Lord Jesus Christ praying always for you. (Colossians 1:3)

We give thanks to God always for you all, making mention of you in our prayers. (1 Thessalonians 1:2)

I thank God, whom I serve from my forefathers with pure conscience, that without ceasing I have

remembrance of thee in my prayers night and
day. (2 Timothy 1:3)

Paul sought The Most High three times about a problem in his
body. And he prayed for others over and over. Do not give up. Both
Jesus and Paul are showing us we are to keep asking until you get an
answer. Whether that answer is yes, no, move on, or this is my will
for you.

In Luke 11:1–10, 18:3–8, Jesus gives us two examples of per-
sistence faith. Please read those now. In one, the word *importunity* is
used. In the other, the word *faith* is used. Importunity means persistent. You keep praying until He shows you your next move. Asking
over and over for the same thing is persistent faith. You cannot weary
The Most High with righteous, persistent prayer.

In Mark 10:46–52, blind Bartimeus would not shut up until
Jesus heard him. The crowd around Bartimeus told him to shut up
and leave Jesus alone. But Bartimeus's persistent faith told him to
keep crying out until he was heard by Jesus.

And he (Jesus) spake a parable unto them to this
end, that men ought always to pray, and not to
faint. (Luke 18:1)

IN JESUS'S NAME

And whatsoever you should ask in my name, that will I do, that the Father may be glorified in the Son. If ye ask anything in my name I will do it. (John 14:13–14)

And in that day you shall ask me nothing verily, verily, I say unto you, whatsoever ye shall ask the Father in my name, he will give it you. Hitherto have you asked nothing in my name: ask, and you shall receive, that your joy may be full. (John 16:23–24)

Did you notice something in the above verses? In John chapter 14, Jesus said, "If ye ask anything in my name I will do it." But notice that in John chapter 16, he says, "Whatsoever you ask The Father in my name, He will do." Do you see the different way it is spoken? Which is correct? Both of them, because Jesus is God!

Then Peter said, silver and gold have I none; But such as I have give I thee: In the name of Jesus Christ of Nazareth rise up and walk. (Acts 3:6)

And his name through faith in his name have made this man strong, whom ye see and know: yea, the faith which is by him (Jesus) have given

> him (the man) this perfect soundness in the pres-
> ence of you all. (Acts 3:16)

> Be it known unto you all, and to all the people
> of Israel, that by the name of Jesus Christ of
> Nazareth, whom ye crucified, whom God raised
> from the dead even by him doth this man stand
> here before you whole. (Acts 4:10)

> And there he found a certain man named Aeneas,
> which had kept his bed eight years, and was sick of
> the palsy. And Peter said unto him, Aeneas, Jesus
> Christ maketh thee whole: arise and make thy
> bed. And he arose immediately. (Acts 9:33–34)

> And this did she many days. But Paul, being
> grieved, turned said to the spirit, I command thee
> in the name of Jesus Christ to come out of her.
> And he came out the same hour. (Acts 16:18)

Jesus is The Most High in flesh. Once that is accepted, other things fall in line. When you "ask in my name," this is not a mantra chant that is to be used over and over. Mantras are used repeatedly in Hinduism, Buddhism, Catholicism, and other mystical religions. Those followers believe that by saying certain words over and over, they will get what they wish. As saints, we have no such mantras. We can ask in Jesus's name, but to do it over and over and over, we have made it into a mantra. The key is to have faith in that holy name.

> And they took the bullock which was given them,
> and they dressed it, and called on the name of
> Baal, from morning even until noon, saying O
> Baal, hear us. But there was no voice, nor any
> that answered. And they leaped upon the altar
> which was made. (1 Kings 18:26)

These worshippers of baal felt he was not hearing them, so they call his name over and over, hoping someone hears. That is a mantra.

> Then certain of the Vagabond Jews, exorcists, took upon them to call over them which had evil spirits the name of the Lord Jesus saying, we adjure you by Jesus whom Paul preacheth. And there were seven sons of one Sceva, a jew, and chief of the priest, which did so. And the evil spirit answered and said Jesus I know, and Paul I know; but who are ye? And the man in whom the evil spirit was leaped on them, overcame them, and prevailed against them, so that they fled out the house naked and wounded. (Acts 19:13–16)

These seven witch doctors used the name of Jesus, but it meant nothing to them because they did not have faith or trust in that holy name. So it was useless to them; Jesus was not their Savior, so they had no right to use His holy name. They were imitating Paul. Saying His name twenty times has no more power than saying it once. There have been times I was in a group and I heard someone pray, and I knew they were not saved, and I would hear that person use the name of Jesus. And it sounded like mockery. You absolutely must have faith in the name of Jesus, which means you must be saved to use His name. Remember we have no exorcist in the church looking for demons to cast out; that is not a spiritual gift (1 Corinthians 12:1–10; Ephesian 4:10–16).

Let me issue a caution. There are times in need I call on the name of Jesus over and over. It is not a mantra but my plea to The Most High for help in a time of need. Just be careful. Jeremiah 10:2 tells us not to learn the way of the heathen or unsaved. It does not matter how good it sounds; ensure it honors The Most High. He wants your joy to be full. So draw near with a true heart in full assurance of faith. Come boldly to the throne of grace!

FASTING

There are times of prayer when more is needed, and you must add fasting. Usually this is associated with demon procession and strong yokes (binding of evil strongholds) of wickedness.

> And He (Jesus) said unto them, this kind can come forth by nothing, but by prayer and fasting. (Mark 9:29)

Fasting means to abstain from food, water, or both. You can also fast anything pleasurable (i.e., sex, sweets). But usually it is food, water, or both. The best definition of fasting is found in Isaiah chapter 58.

> Wherefore have we fasted, say they, and thou seest not? Wherefore have we afflicted our souls, and thou takest no knowledge? Behold, in the day of your fast ye find pleasure, and exact all your laborers. Behold, ye fast for strife and debate, and to smite with the fist of wickedness: ye shall not fast as you do this day, to make your voice to be heard on high. Is it such a fast that I have chosen, a day for man to afflict his soul? Is it to bow down his head as a bulrush, and to spread sackcloth and ashes under him? Wilt thou call this a fast, and an acceptable day of the Lord? Is

not this the fast that I have chosen? To loose the
bands of wickedness, to undo the heavy burdens,
and to let the oppressed go free, that ye break
every yoke. (Isaiah 58:3–6)

The people were complaining that their efforts in fasting were
not producing any results. The Most High then counselled them on
what He considered a true fast, which is to humble and discipline
our body and soul, break bands of wickedness, lift heavy burdens,
and let those who are oppressed by evilness break free. It was not to
be a day of pleasure nor to continue as usual. Fasting was not a time
for showing who was the most spiritual. Fasting should be done in
private, and only those who need to know should be informed. It
can be conducted by a group or church body, but it must be done
in humility and forgoing those things we consider pleasurable for a
season. Fasting must be done in truth and sincerity and not for show.

In those days I Daniel was mourning three full
weeks. I ate no pleasant bread, neither came flesh
nor wine in my mouth, neither did I anoint myself
at all, till three whole weeks were fulfilled…Then
said he unto me, fear not, Daniel: for from the
first day that thou didst set thine heart to understand, and to chasten thyself before thy God, thy
words were heard, and I am come for thy words.
(Daniel 10:2–3, 12)

Daniel sought answers, so he prayed and fasted for three full
weeks (twenty-one days) before the answer came. Notice he chastens
(humbles) himself before The Most High. He said he did not anoint
himself; does that mean he did not take a bath? I am sure he took a
bath because he had to go before the king while doing his work. He
may not have put on any perfume during that time.

Then I proclaimed a fast there, at the river Ahava,
that we might afflict ourselves before our God,

to seek of him a right way for us, and for our little ones, and for all our substance. For I was ashamed to require of the king a band of soldiers and horsemen to help us against the enemy in the way: because we had spoken unto the king, saying, the hand of our God is upon all them for good that seek him; but his power and his wrath is against all them that forsake him. So we fasted and besought our God for this: and he was entreated of us. (Ezra 8:21–23)

Ezra proclaimed a fast to seek protection during their travels to Israel. And The Most High gave them their request. Notice how he bragged on The Most High.

And Jonah began to enter into the city a day's journey, and he cried, and said, yet forty days, and Nineveh shall be overthrown. So, the people of Nineveh believe God and proclaimed a fast, and put on sackcloth, from the greatest of them even to the least of them. For the word came unto the king of Nineveh, and he arose from his throne, and he laid his robe from him, and covered him with sackcloth, and sat in ashes. And he caused it to be proclaimed and published through Nineveh by the decree of the king and his nobles, saying let neither man nor beast, herd nor flock, taste anything: let them not feed, nor drink water: But let man and beast be covered with sackcloth, and cry mightily unto God: yea, let them turn everyone from his evil way, and from the violence that is in their hands. Who can tell if God will turn and repent and turn away from his fierce anger, and we perish not? And God saw their works, that they turned from their evil way; And God repented of the evil, that he

had said that he would do unto them; And he did
it not. (Jonah 3:4–10)

Notice two things here: one, they believed The Most High and proclaimed a national fast. They put on sackcloth and sat in ashes, and they repented of their evil ways. Second, The Most High saw their repentance, and He changed (repented) His mind on punishing them. He did not repent of evil, for there is no evil in our Father. You do not need to put on sackcloth or sit in ashes; this is just an outward symbol of inner humbleness. Just humble your mind (heart), which is most important.

> Moreover when ye fast, be not, as the hypocrites, of a sad countenance: for they disfigure their faces, that they may appear unto men to fast. Verily I say unto you, they have their reward. But thou, when thou fastest, anoint thy head, and wash thy face; That thou appear not unto men to fast, but unto thy Father which is in secret: and thy Father, which seeth in secret, shall reward thee openly. (Matthew 6:16–18)

Most times, a fast should be done in secret without fanfare. Just between you and The Most High. Others need not know, unless it is necessary. Do not let others know you are fasting just to get their approval, for then you have gotten your reward. I have met people who have a sad look on their faces, and you asked them why, and they replied, "I am fasting." They should stop right then and repent, for they have gotten their reward.

A fast can be of any length. Read Deuteronomy chapter 9. Moses did three forty-day fasts, with two of them back-to-back with no food or water in between. What Moses did was enabled by The Most High. I do not recommend an eighty-day fast. It could kill you. Medical doctors believe you can go without food for one or two months. They also say you may be able to go without water for a few days. So be incredibly careful when attempting multiple days of fasting. I have done a few three-day fasts of food and water, but I did drink fruit juice for those three days. Be careful if you take certain medications; do not just skip your doses. Do not walk around with a sad face, letting others know you are fasting. You have your reward, their admiration.

Luke 2:36–38 tells us that Anna served The Most High, day and night, with her prayers and fasting.

This does not mean you need to go live in a convent to serve the Lord. But shows a commitment to prayer. Many equate fasting with casting out demons, and that is partially correct. Fasting is not just for casting out demons, as you can see from the above verses.

Every sin or sickness is not a sign of demon possession, as some teach. Let me repeat this: "Every sin or sickness is not a sign of demon possession." There is no demon of colds, flu, cancer, or heart disease, nor is there a group of sexual demons. Any demon can try to influence you into any sin, including sexual sins.

> But every man is tempted, when he is drawn away of his own lust, and enticed. Then when lust hath conceived, it bringeth forth sin: and sin, when it is finished, bringeth forth death. (James 1:14–15)

As you can see, there is no sexual demon. Any demon can try to draw you away using your own lust to entice you to sin.

> But those things which proceed out of the mouth come forth from the heart (mind): and they defile the man. For out of the heart proceed evil *thoughts*, murders, adulteries, fornications, thefts, false witness, blasphemies: These are the things which defile a man: but to eat with unwashen hands defileth not a man. (Matthew 15:18–20)

> Thefts, covetousness, wickedness, deceit, lasciviousness, an evil eye, blasphemy, pride, foolish-

ness; all these evil things come from within and defile the man. (Mark 7:22–23)

Notice that it says evil thoughts. Your heart cannot think. Thoughts come from the mind, which resides in the brain. Our enemy works on fleshly lusts (Galatians 5:17–21) to entice you to sin. Whether that is sexual, food, stealing, or pride. Even if you are saved, demons try to entice you to sin. They cannot make you sin but entice you to sin.

MENTAL ILLNESS

. . . .

Most of us are not spiritually mature enough to discern between mental illness and demon possession. You must be incredibly careful in this area of mental illness. A wrong diagnosis could lead to catastrophic results. You may need to refer that person for psychoanalysis for evaluation. This is not a lack of faith but reality. In this fallen world, there are mental health issues. I would rather err on the side of caution.

And Jesus went about all Galilee, teaching in their synagogues, and preaching the gospel of the Kingdom, healing all manner of sickness and all manner of diseases among the people. And his fame went throughout all Syria: and they bought unto him all sick people that were taken with divers diseases and torments, and those which were possessed with devils, and those which were lunatic, and those that had the palsy; and he healed them. (Matthew 4:23–24)

And when even was come, they brought unto him many that were possessed with devils: and

> he cast out the spirits with his word, and healed
> all that were sick. (Matthew 8:16)

As you can see, not everyone had demons; some were just sick, lunatic, or the palsy, which is a type of being paralyzed.

Let me give a warning to those who say they have the gift of discerning spirits (1 Corinthians 12:10). This gift is very easily abused. It is easy to get into judgementalism. I am not talking about judging right and wrong; we are to do that. But having an attitude that nothing is right unless you say it is right is *judgementalism*. Be careful.

Nowhere in the Bible do we find saints whose sole job was to find demon-possessed people and set them free. No saint can be demon-possessed. All saints are oppressed by demons; they are our enemies. We should seek The Most High and not devils. Do not spend much of your time reading about demons. It is a confusing area of study, and most of what is written by teachers is wrong. We are commanded to study God not the devil and demons.

Let me give one more area of caution. Do not read the many fictional books on so-called spiritual warfare: The *Harry Potter* series by J. K. Rowling; *The Lord of the Rings* and *The Hobbit* by J. R. R. Tolkien; *Chronicles of Narnia: The Lion, The Witch, and The Wardrobe* book series and *The Screwtape Letters* by C. S. Lewis. All of these books used witchcraft to teach about The Most High. Tolkien and Lewis would get together over a cold beer to talk spiritual matters (*The Literary Traveler,* October 2006). So who did the talking: them or the beer?

> And have no fellowship with the unfruitful works
> of darkness, but rather reprove them. (Ephesians
> 5:11)

Witchcraft in any form is of the flesh and demonic (Galatians 5:18–21). We should not read books written by earthly authors on this subject. A lie is the only thing satan will teach us about The Most

High. Many Christian leaders push these types of books because they are entertaining. Do not read any of them.

> Finally, brethren, whatsoever things are true, whatsoever things are honest, whatsoever things are just, whatsoever things are pure, whatsoever things are lovely, whatsoever things are of good report; If there be any virtue, if there be any praise, think on these things. (Philippians 4:8)

If I am reading the above verse correctly, we should not read fiction. Fiction is nothing more than fantasy. Ladies, this includes so-called fictional Christian romance novels.

One more thing before we move on. I can find nowhere in scripture that tells us to use oil in casting out demons. If it is there, I cannot find it. We are to use fasting and prayer (Mark 6:13).

PRAYING IN TONGUES

This is the last subject we shall cover in this study. Should we pray in tongues? Many Christians think when they are praying in what they believe are tongues, their prayers are really working. But this is a misconception and wrong interpretation of scriptures. I am not going to give a thorough study of praying in tongues but enough to help you in your own study.

> There are, it may be so many kinds of voices in the world, none of them is without signification. Therefore, if I know not the meaning of the voice, I should be unto him that speaketh a barbarian, and he that speaketh shall be a barbarian unto me. Even so you, for as much as you are zealous of spiritual gifts, seek that you may excel to the edifying of the church. Wherefore let him that speaketh in an unknown tongue pray that he may interpret. For if I pray in an unknown tongue, my spirit prayeth, but my understanding is unfruitful. What is it then? I will pray with the spirit, I will pray with the understanding also: I will sing with the spirit, and I will sing with the understanding also. Else when thou shalt bless with the spirit (tongues), how shall he that occupy the room of the unlearned say Amen at thy giving of thanks, seeing he understandeth not

what thou sayest? For thou verily giveth thanks well, but the other is not edified. I think my God, I speak with tongues more than you all: yet in the church I had rather speak five words with my understanding, that by my voice I might teach others also, than ten thousand words in an unknown tongue. (1 Corinthians 14:10–19)

Tongues were not meant to teach believers; rather, tongues were given as a sign for the unbelievers (Acts 2:1–11) so that they would hear the words of The Most High in their languages. It was not for believers to impress each other as to who was the most spiritual. The church has turned tongues into a circus. If you pay attention to those speaking in tongues, they all sound alike, and it is very repetitive. But if you read Acts chapter 2, the visitors (nonbelievers) heard the Christians speak the wonderful works of God in their own individual languages: Parthians, Medes, Elamites, Mesopotamia, etc.

Understand this: Paul went to many foreign places, even though he did not know many different languages. He needed to be able to speak a few languages he had not learned, and that is where the ability to speak in tongues or foreign languages helped. He was given this ability by The Most High to enable the gospel to be spread.

How can you pray for those things we have been told to pray for if you do not know what you are saying? I am not knocking the use of tongues, but the church has corrupted the true meaning of tongues. And I believe when in doubt, leave it alone until you get a better understanding. Tongues are one spiritual gift that cannot be refuted by someone saying you are not saying anything. Because it is up to the speaker of the tongues to decide if it is true. If you really want a spiritual gift, seek the absolute best spiritual gift (1 Corinthians 12:27–1,13:1–13), and that is love. Love is the greatest spiritual gift. The purpose of all gifts are to edify the church.

CONCLUSION

There are times when our prayers for healing are not answered. During those times, we must trust The Most High and lean not to our own understanding. Paul prayed three times to be released from a thorn in his flesh (2 Corinthians 12:1–10). Whatever the thorn was, he did not get deliverance. For thirteen years, I have suffered with fistulas (holes in my abdominal skin area, with fluid coming from my intestines) as a result of being shot. I do not know why I am not fully healed yet. But I trust in my Father that He knows best. I take seriously what was written to Paul.

> And he said unto me, My grace is sufficient for thee; for my strength is made perfect in weakness. Most gladly therefore will I rather glory in my infirmities, that the power of Christ may rest upon me. (2 Corinthians 12:9)

What are you to do if you are not healed? You continue to serve and worship Him. Nothing says you will never get sick or will always be healed. He is sovereign. He cares for us, but there are times when we will not get healed. I am not here to make excuses for The Most High. I do not know why everyone does not get healing. I would like to be healed from those six bullets, but I trust my Father; He is going to work this out for my good, for His glory. And in heaven, I will not have this frail and broken body. Hallelujah, amen.

I had a few so-called friends who told me I must have committed a big sin to get shot six times. I no longer bother with those people. Because they do not have knowledge of The Most High. Suffering is not always a sign of sin in your life. Suffering is usually a sign of being a partaker of Christ's suffering (1 Peter chapters 2 and 4). Most of the time when I pray, I never mention what is wrong with me. I want to communicate with my Father. When we read what The Most High told Paul upon Paul's conversion in Acts 9:15–16, we love the part where Paul was told he is a "chosen vessel," but we miss verse 16 where Paul was told, "For I will show him how great things he must suffer for my name's sake."

Paul did not get healed (2 Corinthians 12:1–10). Timothy did not get healed (1 Timothy 5:23). You can get to heaven after suffering a sickness, but you cannot get there without salvation. Beware of those super-faith folks who know why everyone else does not get healed. They will tell you there is secret sin in your life. And there may be, but how do they know—have they been to a heavenly meeting? Jesus has taken the wrath of The Most High and given us salvation (1 Thessalonians 5:9).

We all know what is in ourselves, and we must examine ourselves before The Most High. There are some things that should be common sense. Habits we develop can cause sickness. If you are a user of tobacco, expect cancer. If you take drugs and abuse those drugs, you will get addicted. There are studies (MUSC) that show no one should drink alcoholic beverages, especially women; a little alcoholic drink per day can cause breast cancer, cirrhosis of the liver, or early death. There is an ongoing debate in Christian circles about the use of alcoholic beverages by Christians. I find that wherever alcoholic beverages were used, excess was there. Why would anyone support anything that has caused such pain and destruction? Plus, it is a work of the flesh with no redeeming value. Read Galatians 5:17–22.

Overeating and excessive weight and not getting any exercise can cause problems. Some saints can hardly walk because of excessive weight. Our bodies were not made to carry around all this gospel bird (fried chicken) and cakes. Saints want to abuse their bodies, then pray The Most High heals the consequences of their abuse.

There is more than enough sickness in this world without us voluntarily seeking more.

> For bodily exercise profiteth little; but godliness
> is profitable unto all things, having a promise of
> the life that now is and of that which is to come.
> (1 Timothy 4:8)

Exercise does help a little, whereas no exercise does not help at all. But godliness (salvation) should keep you from a lot of hurtful things now and get you into heaven. And remember, prayer is for communication with our Father, not just for healing.

You do not have to be the bearer of bad news. Before you tell someone that they are suffering because of their sin, ensure The Most High is asking you to speak that truth into their lives.

DOES THE MOST HIGH
STILL SPEAK

· · · ·

Does The Most High still speak today in an audible voice? I hear many saints say He speaks to them and carries on a conversation with them. They think He is speaking to them in that manner, but I am not here to dispute that.

In the Old Testament, The Most High spoke to many different people using prophets, angels, and even His own voice. The Most High can do whatever He wishes too, in any manner He wants. He speaks to us by placing thoughts in our minds and through His Bible. He also speaks through dreams and visions, but you must be careful with dreams because we can make ourselves dream.

> For thus saith the Lord of hosts, the God of Israel;
> Let not your prophets and your diviners, that be
> in the midst of you, deceive you, neither hearken

to your dreams which ye cause to be dreamed.
(Jeremiah 29:8)

God who at sundry times and in divers manners
spake in time past unto the fathers by the prophets, Hath in these last days spoken unto us by his
Son, whom he hath appointed heir of all things, by
whom also he made the worlds. (Hebrews 1:1–2)

For if the word spoken by angels was steadfast, and every transgression and disobedience
received a just recompense or reward; How shall
we escape, if we neglect so great salvation: which
at the first began to be spoken by the Lord, and
was confirmed unto us by them that heard him?
(Hebrews 2:2–3)

In the New Testament, Jesus has spoken to all that we need. If you
never hear the voice of The Most High, Jesus has given us all we need. If
a situation arises and you cannot find an answer, then you must:

And whatsoever ye do in word or deed, do all in
the name of the Lord Jesus, giving thanks to God
and the Father by him. (Colossians 3:17)

Whether therefore ye eat, or drink, or whatsoever
ye do, do all to the glory of God. (1 Corinthians
10:31)

Many Christians agonize over what His will is for their lives.
Unless He gives you something specific, just ensuring whatever you
do brings Him glory and honor, you are doing His will for your life
or situation. Sitting and waiting on Him does nothing. You must do
as a waiter' they wait or serve a table. Do what you know to do until
you get further instructions. Ensuring that whatever you do gives
Him glory, you are in His will.

In Matthew 16:13–23, Peter spoke what our Father had given him, and Jesus commended Peter for speaking that which was given to him by The Most High. And then Peter spoke what was given to him by satan, and Jesus rebuked him. So be careful what you hear; ensure it is from our Father and not from your mind or satan. The Most High will never contradict the Bible, His word.

DO NOT TRUST YOUR HEART

The heart is deceitful above all things and desperately wicked: who can know it? I the Lord search the heart, I try the reins, even to give every man according to his ways, and according to the fruit of his doing. (Jeremiah 17:9–10)

But those things which proceed out of the mouth come forth from the heart and they defile the man. For out of the heart proceed evil thoughts, murder, adulteries, fornication, thefts, false witness, blasphemies: These are the things which defile a man: but to eat with unwashen hands defileth not a man. (Matthew 15:18–20)

A good man out of the good treasure of his heart bringeth forth that which is good: and an evil man out of the evil treasure of his heart bringeth forth that which is evil; for of the abundance of the heart his mouth speaketh. (Luke 6:45)

This is why we must:

Trust in the Lord with all thine heart; and lean not unto thine on understanding. In all thy ways acknowledge him, and he shall direct thy paths.

> Be not wise in thine own eyes: fear the Lord, and
> depart from evil. (Proverbs 3:5–7)

> I will worship toward thy holy temple, and praise
> thy name for thy loving-kindness and for thy
> truth: for thou hast magnified thy word above all
> thy name. (Psalm 138:2)

This means The Most High has magnified His word, the Bible, above His holy name. The Bible is all we have, so He will ensure it is the truth and the life.

> But therein is the righteousness of God revealed
> from faith to faith: as it is written, The just shall
> live by faith. (Romans 1:17)

Each of us must answer this holy call to prayer. It is not an option; there is no excuse. I have missed the mark in my prayer life. Let us repent. If you are not praying, it is time to repent and get to work. Start small, a few minutes at a time. And as you mature, your prayer time will increase. Studying the Bible is a must in developing a prayer life. You must have faith, for without faith it is impossible to please or come to The Most High (Hebrews 11:6). Do not get routine in your prayer life. The goal of this work is to encourage each of us to pray in season, pray out of season, and after you have done all, then pray even more. If you are a saint and are not praying, you are in violation (sin) of a command (men ought always pray).

I have written against many cherished traditions. It is not my goal to destroy or bring in confusion, but to bring clarity to our prayer life. Please study your Bible and see if what I have written is true.

> These were more noble than those in Thessalonica,
> in that they receive the word with all readiness of
> mind, and searched the scriptures daily, whether
> those things were so. (Acts 17:11)

For the eyes of the Lord are over the righteous, and his ears are open unto their prayers: but the face of the Lord is against them that do evil. (1 Peter 3:12)

Humble yourselves in the sight of the Lord, and he shall lift you up. (James 4:10)

Humble yourselves therefore under the mighty hand of God, that he may exalt you in due time: casting all your care upon him: for he careth for you. (1 Peter 5:6–7)

What shall we then say to these things? If God be for us, who can be against us? He that spared not his own Son, but delivered him up for us all, how shall he not with him also freely give us all things? Who is he that condemneth? It is Christ that died, yea rather, that is risen again, who is even at the right hand of God, who also maketh intercession for us. Who shall separate us from the love of Christ? Shall tribulation or distress, or persecution, or famine, or nakedness, or peril, or sword? As it is written, for thy sake we are killed all the day long; we are accounted as sheep for the slaughter. Nay, in all these things we are more than conquerors through him that loved us. For I am persuaded, that neither death, nor life, nor angels, nor principalities, nor power, nor things present, nor things to come, nor height, nor depth, nor any other creature, shall be able to separate us from the love of God, which is in Christ Jesus our Lord. (Romans 8:31–39)

Rejoicing in hope; patient in tribulation; continuing in prayer. (Romans 12:12)

But the end of all things is at hand: be ye sober, and watch unto prayer. (1 Peter 4:7)

Now unto Him that is able to do exceeding abundantly above all that we ask or think, according to the power that worketh in us, unto Him be glory in the church by Christ Jesus throughout all ages, world without end. Amen. (Ephesians 3:20–21)

The sacrifice of the wicked is an abomination to the Lord: but the prayer of the upright is his delight. (Proverbs 15:8)

Please take what I have written and examine it through the eyes of scripture.
Always remember:
The Most High is sovereign.
He is just.
He is full of compassion.
He will always do that which is right.
Nothing is too hard for Him.
We are in the last days. Let us become The Most High's peculiar people—a people of prayer. Amen. And remember that the Bible ends with a prayer.

He which testifieth these things saith, Surely, I come quickly. Amen. Even so, come Lord Jesus, the grace of our Lord Jesus Christ be with you all. Amen. (Revelation 22:20–22)

Jesus is coming back!
Are you ready?

ABOUT THE AUTHOR

Minister Robert Johnson has been a student of the Bible for over forty years. His life verse is 2 Timothy 2:16: "Study to show thyself approved unto God, a workman that needeth not to be ashamed, rightly dividing the word of truth." He employs a systematic two-year study of the Bible, which he does over and over. This time frame does not include time studying and preparing sermons.

His goal has always been to learn more about The Most High and to cut through the useless traditions the church loves. A large number of traditions the church teaches are not based on scripture. They are based on fables, superstitions, and the commandments of men. His goal is to endorse nothing the Bible does not plainly teach. Minister Johnson is also the author of *The Spirit of the Anti-Christ*. A book on the end-time world leader called the antichrist. He is also the author of *On Point!: The Making of a Prison Contraband Captain*. A book on why the leadership of the prison gang (Crips) wanted him dead. They paid an ex-inmate $6,000.00 to assassinate him.

On Point demonstrates some of the principles taught in this book on prayer.